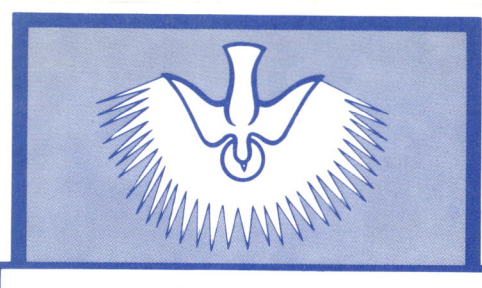

This Book
has been presented to the
CHURCH LIBRARY
of Hester Shortridge

Memorial Library

by Mrs. William Kirsch, Jr.

PUTTING YOUR LIFE ON THE LINE

Maurice A. Fetty

ABINGDON
Nashville

PUTTING YOUR LIFE ON THE LINE

Copyright © 1977 by Abingdon

All rights reserved.
No part of this book may be reproduced in any manner whatsoever without written permission of the publisher except brief quotations embodied in critical articles or reviews. For information address Abingdon, Nashville, Tennessee.

Library of Congress Cataloging in Publication Data

Fetty, Maurice A 1936-
  Putting your life on the line.

  1. Lenten sermons. 2. Congregational churches—Sermons. 3. Sermons, American. I. Title.
BV4277.F47   252'.62   76-43351

ISBN 0-687-34945-1

Scripture quotations noted RSV are from the Revised Standard Version Common Bible, copyrighted © 1973.

Scripture quotations noted NEB are from the New English Bible, copyright © the Delegates of the Oxford University Press and the Syndics of the Cambridge University Press, 1961, 1970.

Lines on pp. 57-58, 69 are from "The Fool on the Hill" (John Lennon/Paul McCartney) © 1967 Northern Songs Limited. All rights for the United States, Canada, Mexico, and the Philippines controlled by Comet Music Corp. c/o ATV Music Group. Used by permission. All rights reserved.

Poetry on pp. 84-85 is from "The Hollow Men" in *Collected Poems 1909-1962* by T. S. Eliot, copyright, 1936, by Harcourt Brace Jovanovich, Inc.; copyright © 1963, 1964, by T. S. Eliot. Reprinted by permission of the publishers Harcourt Brace Jovanovich, Inc. and Faber and Faber Ltd.

Poetry on p. 83, from Edwin Markham's "The Unbelievable," is used by permission of the Markham Archives.

Quotation on pp. 24-25 from "Downtown," words and music by Tony Hatch, © Copyright 1964 by Welbeck Music, Ltd., London, England. Sole Selling Agent MCA Music, a Division of MCA, Inc., 445 Park Ave., New York, N.Y. 10022 for North, South and Central America. Used by permission. All rights reserved.

Selection on pp. 59-60 from *Trial Before Pilate,* lyrics by Tim Rice, Music by Andrew Lloyd Webber, © Copyright 1970 by Leeds Music Ltd., London, England. Sole Selling Agent Leeds Music Corporation, 445 Park Ave., New York, N.Y. for North, South and Central America. Used by permission. All rights reserved.

MANUFACTURED BY THE PARTHENON PRESS AT
NASHVILLE, TENNESSEE, UNITED STATES OF AMERICA

To My Father and Mother,
Clifford and Eva Fetty

Preface

All the world is a stage, and as actors upon it we have our roles to play, with their entrances and exits. So observed Shakespeare with his characteristic astuteness. To a considerable extent, heredity and environment have given us the context and means by which we play out our roles. There is little we can do to change that. But we are able to decide what we do with what we have been given. We may or may not rise to the challenges of our time. We may or may not attempt to fulfill our potential. We may or may not be aware of the significance of our role.

If life is a drama, it is to many a melodrama. Others see it as comedy or tragedy or both. Some regard it as a joke, a farce, a big put-on. Others see life cynically as illusion or futility or, as Shakespeare observed, as a

PUTTING YOUR LIFE ON THE LINE

tale told by an idiot, full of sound and fury signifying nothing. Consequently it has become common for people to play their parts as sham actors, as hypocrites, as characters who play a role but never get into it. Therefore, you never really know who they are or where they stand.

Jesus stands in contrast to hypocrisy and futility. He was impatient with self-serving religious institutionalism. Pretension and self-righteousness received his scorn. He called men and women to a life of authenticity by asking them to put their lives on the line, to take up their crosses and follow him.

Though he was aware of the tragicomedy of life, he took his role seriously and would not relinquish it even in the face of death. His courage and authenticity breathe new excitement into life. His victory reassures us life is not in vain.

His call to put our lives on the line is not easy, but it is authentic. And it is refreshing and rewarding, for once we really get into his act, we begin to understand what the play is all about.

Contents

A New Kind of Teaching 11
Three Levels of Discipleship 23
The High Cost of Loving 34
Jesus and the Deserters 47
The Fool on the Hill 57
The Problem of Authority in Religion 70
The Message of Death vs. the Gospel of Life 83

A New Kind of Teaching
Mark 1:21-28

Teachers and teaching have been with us since the world began. Early man taught his children how to survive—how to hunt, how to plant and harvest, how to provide shelter and protection, how to fight, how to raise his family in the tribal ways.

Learning and teaching took a great stride forward in classical Greece, four hundred fifty years before Christ, with the arrival of Socrates and his brilliant student Plato. The radiant light of learning was passed on from Plato to Aristotle, and the world ever since has been their beneficiary.

Teaching and learning declined in the so-called Dark Ages and medieval period only to be revived by the Renaissance, the Reformation, and the Enlighten-

PUTTING YOUR LIFE ON THE LINE

ment. Public schools, colleges, and universities began to proliferate across the landscape of Western civilization to cause the general educational level to rise like a giant tide lifting all of life to a higher plane.

Only a few short years ago education was an option in this country, but now it is law. And in this great nation we have more students in college or university than ever before anywhere in history. Learning is a way of life; teaching, an honored and powerful profession.

But it is a profession increasingly difficult. Some believe a college is best defined as a log with an earnest student on one end and a brilliant, sympathetic teacher on the other. Others scoff at such simplistic notions as they proudly point to their highly technical learning laboratories and complex information retrieval systems.

Not only is educational theory debated, educational practice is positively staggering. Think for a moment of the amount of information available. Our federal government, for example, generates 100,000 reports each year, in addition to 450,000 articles, books, and papers. Who on earth reads all that? Add to that the 60,000,000 pages a year of scientific and technical literature produced in the world plus the 365,000 books written annually, and you have an absolutely overwhelming amount of information. Furthermore, the information, the amount of knowledge, doubles every 10 to 14 years.

A NEW KIND OF TEACHING

Who on earth is going to sort all that out? How are they going to decide what to leave out? Who will teach it and how? Furthermore, what possible relevance does Jesus, a somewhat archaic Galilean teacher of nineteen hundred years ago, have for us today amid all our new information? Years ago his hearers were amazed at what he had to say and remarked that he taught them as one having authority, not as the scribes and Pharisees. They all recognized it as a new kind of teaching.

Even amid the avalanche of information today, I believe his words still come across as a new kind of teaching, and Jesus as a new kind of teacher.

I

For one thing Jesus' teaching was new because it involved *commitment,* not just *comment.*

You probably remember the old definition of a lecture as the process wherein the information in the professor's notes is transferred to the students' notebooks without going through the minds of either. That often is the case with teaching that is mere commentary. It, like the old scribes and Pharisees, assumes that truth is to be found only in the musty pages of the past. Consequently, teaching degenerates into a boring recitation of what someone else thought years ago, adding a little here, subtracting a little there.

Many teachers are mere technicians of information, rearranging facts and opinions in new ways without ever taking a stand existentially, saying, "Here is where I stand; here is where I stake my life." Colleges, universities, and graduate schools can become mere junctions of information and dispatchers of knowledge without ever being creative and existential, and thus authoritative.

When Martin Luther began publishing abroad his new teaching, the time came for him to take a stand and he took it. The gentle and scholarly Erasmus advocated many of the same ideas as Luther, but he had not the courage to take his stand so boldly. Scholars sometimes quip, somewhat inaccurately, that Luther hatched the egg Erasmus laid! Nevertheless, when Luther was called before all the ecclesiastical and political power of medieval Europe to answer for his teachings, as to whether they were his, he replied: "I am bound by the Scriptures I have quoted and my conscience is captive to the Word of God. I cannot and I will not recant anything, for to go against conscience is neither right nor safe. God help me. Here I stand, I cannot do otherwise. Amen." No wonder Luther's teaching had a ring of authority heard all over the world. He staked his life on it.

Amid the blizzard of information available today, you can be sure we are on to something significant when the teacher begins to stake his reputation, even his life, on it. Talk is one thing, but commitment to the subject matter of the talk is quite another.

As in Luther, so in Jesus we have a man who takes a

A NEW KIND OF TEACHING

stand on what he is saying. Many of the scribes and Pharisees of Jesus' time taught dogmatically, which is to say, out of a rigid past and an unimaginative present. Consequently, even though they taught dogmatically, they did not teach authoritatively, because they were not themselves existentially involved. They did not really enter into the situation. They gave stale, textbook answers. The hard, agonizing questions of life were referred to superficial solutions of the past, the pat approaches of a dry faith.

Not so with Jesus. He took the risk, entered into the situation, moved beyond the outdated rigidities, and spoke to the present need with clarity, insight, and conviction. When he spoke, you knew he was sincere and not just mouthing the party line. You had the feeling that if necessary he would stake his life on what he was saying. He was not just a spectator-commentator observing the news. He was committed to making the news. His was a new kind of teaching.

II

Note further, Jesus' teaching had authority because he regarded his hearers with *concern*, not with *contempt*.

Once in awhile when I am out of the city someone will suggest I record my sermon in advance to be played on Sunday. Imagine that! I never do because I always am reminded of a cartoon I once saw. The first panel of the cartoon showed a professor lecturing to a full classroom. The next picture shows a full classroom of students, but no professor. In his place is a tape recorder, giving his words of wisdom for the day. In the next picture the professor's recorder is again giving out his lecture, but this time in place of a roomful of students, we have a roomful of students' tape recorders impersonally recording the impersonal lecture!

College and university students of today have suffered considerably from lack of exposure to top-notch teachers who personally care about them. Frequently students will enroll in certain institutions to study under their renowned authorities, only to discover they rarely, if ever, see them. Usually they are left to the devices of an unknown graduate assistant, or they listen to the outstanding authority along with six hundred other students in the once-a-week lecture series. Frequently our best scholars are caught up in research and publishing, with little personal contact or apparent concern for their students.

Other scholars show contempt for their learners by being as obscure as possible. They teach in riddles and play games to make learning unnecessarily difficult. This very often exhibits the defensiveness and insecurity of the professor. He may be threatened by the brilliance of his students and thus cloak his limited knowledge in pretentious sophistication.

Jesus never played those kinds of games with people. Rather he manifested a deep concern for all

A NEW KIND OF TEACHING

who would learn from him. He used simple stories drawn from the experiences of daily life to illustrate his deepest truths. He exhibited far more concern for the message of the kingdom than for his reputation. Far from withdrawing to an inner circle of intellectual elitism, he ventured out into the countryside and marketplaces and synagogues to make known his views. He loved people and wanted to help them, so he spoke as plainly as possible. No wonder, then, that "the common people heard him gladly."

Almost all disciplines of learning have their own jargon. Technicians, doctors, economists, lawyers, theologians, and ministers have their in-group language. A man once told me he never could figure out what ministers were talking about until he studied a little philosophy. Admittedly, some sermons sound like an insurance policy or legal contract. You never are quite sure what has been said. Perhaps we all withdraw into the security and protection of our businesses and professions because we are afraid and want to protect our corner on things by being obscure.

But Jesus' teaching had a ring of authority, a newness, because he was concerned about his hearers. He wanted them to understand, to know, to learn. So concerned was he that he risked himself, shared himself with his audience. No phony manipulation on his part. No false, gimmicky tricks to get his people to open up while he remained closed. Rather, with him we find a genuine openness, an inner confidence. When we listen to him, we encounter an authentic person, not a shifty, money-grubbing writer of pseudo books. No wonder his was a new kind of teaching. It was the authority of his whole loving person behind it.

As New Testament scholar B. Harvie Branscomb puts it: "Herein was Jesus' contribution—himself. By virtue of the fact that he embodied his ideal, what he said was living and vital and impelling. For religion is a personal thing. It can never become an abstract principle. It is a way of life" *(The Teachings of Jesus* [New York and Nashville: Abingdon Press, 1931], p. 368). Seeing his hearers as sheep without a shepherd, he gave himself to them. He communicated personally his love and compassion.

III

Once again Jesus taught with authority in his kind of teaching because he had a *cure* for the demons, not just *consolation*.

It has not been popular to think of the reality of the demonic until recent years with movies like *Rosemary's Baby* and *The Exorcist,* which drew record crowds. Jesus took the demonic seriously, as do some present-day psychoanalysts. Rollo May says, "The daimonic is *any natural function which has the power to take over the whole person.* Sex and eros, anger and rage, and the craving for power are examples." Today we sometimes would call demon possession by

A NEW KIND OF TEACHING

the word "psychosis." "The daimonic," says Dr. May, "becomes evil when it usurps the total self without regard to the integration of that self" *(Love and Will* [New York: W. W. Norton, 1969], p. 123).

The demoniac Jesus encountered in the Nazareth synagogue was possessed perhaps by a number of demons—demons of hate, guilt, rejection, passion, revenge. As often is the case with demoniacs, his sensibilities and perceptions were greatly heightened, almost to the point of a divine madness. Consequently, upon seeing Jesus, he shrieked, "What do you want with us, Jesus of Nazareth? Have you come to destroy us? I know who you are—the Holy One of God" (Mark 1:24 NEB). Deeply conscious of the inner workings of the psyche, Jesus named the demon, establishing power over him, and ordered him out of the man. Thus the man was at peace.

In William Golding's book and movie, *Lord of the Flies,* a number of small boys are the sole survivors of a shipwreck on a remote island. In their effort to survive, they soon develop a society, rather primitive in form. Evil soon becomes an experienced reality. An old decaying pig's head, surrounded with worms and flies, becomes for them a deity, a god, a "Lord of the Flies," which, retranslated, means "Beelzebub," the "Prince of Darkness and Decay."

A number of the stranded boys, giving full play to their fears and imaginations, soon paint their faces and revert to savagery. In a heightened frenzy during a

PUTTING YOUR LIFE ON THE LINE

nighttime thunderstorm, they kill Simon, whom they mistake for the Beast. Later, Piggy, the intellectual, is killed, as the boys resort more and more to primitive tribalism.

With the power of the demonic in full force, the boys begin to hunt Ralph, the sole survivor of reason and sanity. The frightening chase finally leads out to the beach. Fleeing for his life, and losing, Ralph runs abruptly into a strong, clean, well-built man. The rescue party had arrived, and the demons were halted. Order and love and sensibility had arrived just in time. By the authority of sanity and civilization, the demons were repelled, and Ralph was saved as were the other boys.

Mankind, stranded on this space island, has done its share of sacrificing to demons—the demons of war, hate, revenge, perverted sex, unbridled lust for power, uncontrolled greed, distorted ambition. Like Ralph, many of us have been running desperately along the beaches of the world hoping against hope for the arrival of a rescue party.

As Christians, we now can announce that the rescue party has arrived in the person of the strong man, Jesus. Balanced, integrated, imbued with power, he calls the demons by name, thwarts their power, casts them out, bringing peace out of our demonic frenzy. And for all who submit themselves to his teaching he casts out the demons, calling them by name—fear, guilt, envy, jealousy, lust, negativism, slander, deceit,

A NEW KIND OF TEACHING

revenge, greed. Uncontrolled, these demons will destroy life on this beautiful island in space.

Sociology, history, philosophy, and psychology have a certain kind of power, but not the power of Jesus. Other teachings have authority but not the authority of Jesus' new teaching. Other intellectual disciplines give us self-knowledge, but the more clearly we see ourselves, the more we understand our powerlessness to realize our true aspirations, says Swiss psychiatrist Paul Tournier. "Then it is no longer of healing alone that man stands in need, but of Salvation, of the assurance that the world and he have been redeemed," says Tournier (*The Meaning of Persons* [New York: Harper, 1957], pp. 110-11). We believe Jesus brings that new kind of teaching, the authority of salvation, wholeness, health, and fulfillment.

One time a woman came to me to talk about her son in college. He had been getting involved with a rather conservative Christian campus group, and she was worried, fearing the kind of Christianity they were teaching. I advised patience, believing more good than harm would result.

Sometime later we talked again. An unbelievable change had come over her son. Whereas once he had been, in her words, a little spoiled rich kid obsessed with his own selfish concerns, he now was generous, thoughtful, outgoing, and determined to help others.

What had happened? He had fallen under the spell

PUTTING YOUR LIFE ON THE LINE

of a new kind of teaching, the teaching of Christ. The demons of selfishness, contempt, and greed had been cast out by the authority of Christ. He was a new man, and now he is helping make a new world as a missionary.

It is a new kind of teaching—a teaching with commitment, not just comment; concern, not contempt; cure for your demons and mine, not just consolation.

Three Levels of Discipleship
Luke 6:43-49

The word "disciple" comes from a word which means "to grasp, to take hold of." Thus a disciple is one who grasps or takes hold of a teacher and his teaching. "Discipline" comes from the same root. A disciple, therefore, is a learning, disciplined follower of a leader or teacher.

During his lifetime, Jesus had a wide assortment of disciples. Many were surprising. Some whom we would have expected to be very good actually were not, and some whom we might have expected to be very bad actually were among the best.

Our text reveals, almost incidentally, three levels of

PUTTING YOUR LIFE ON THE LINE

discipleship of those associated with Jesus. Time has moved on since the days of the original disciples, but the problem of three-level discipleship still remains.

I

The first-level disciples are those who merely *come* to Christ, and nothing more.

People who know something about crowds realize they comprise many persons who are there because they like to be with crowds. It serves as an antidote to loneliness and the feeling of insignificance. Consequently, we cluster together in crowded cities, packed subways, and jammed freeways, partly at least because we feel we are where the action is if we are with the crowd.

Are you feeling neglected and alone and bored? Then, in the words of the popular song, go downtown.

> When you're alone and life is making you lonely,
> You can always go Downtown.
> When you've got worries, all the noise and
>   the hurry seems to help, I know, Downtown.
> Just listen to the music of the traffic in the city.
> Linger on the sidewalk where the neon signs
>   are pretty. How can you lose?
> The lights are much brighter there,
> You can forget all your troubles, forget
>   all your cares,
> So go Downtown, things'll be great when
>   you're Downtown.

THREE LEVELS OF DISCIPLESHIP

No finer place, for sure, Downtown.
Everything's waiting for you, Downtown.
(Tony Hatch)

Get with the crowd, you'll feel better. Rub elbows with people, and you'll feel more a part of it. Observers of the Times Square New Year's Eve crowd say many people go there for the sole purpose of pressing up close to another human being, especially one of the opposite sex. Feeling lonely and blue, they go downtown. Why did some people come to Jesus? They wanted to be a part of the crowd, a part of the action.

Others probably came to Jesus because they wanted to see a celebrity, to draw off strength and prestige from his charisma. Insignificant themselves, many people feel greatly enhanced if they can be near a famous person. For a brief moment they can dream of themselves as important personages. Perhaps some of the aura and glamour will wear off on them. Some people came to Jesus for those reasons, and still do.

Others come to the celebrity crowd to see and be seen. They do not care all that much for the celebrity, but they do like the fact that he has the power to attract a crowd and thus give them a social setting in which to flaunt themselves and to catch up on the latest gossip.

Of course, in Russia and China, Jesus rarely attracts that kind of crowd. He has little celebrity status there. Few would take the risk of being seen with him under

PUTTING YOUR LIFE ON THE LINE

any circumstances. But in first-century Palestine and twentieth-century America, we have a different situation. It is all right, sometimes even to our great advantage, to be seen in a Jesus-crowd. Under circumstances of that kind, many of us come to Jesus.

But associating with Jesus on that basis is a very low level of discipleship, if indeed it is discipleship at all. Any knowledgable leader realizes he really cannot count on social butterflies and celebrity crowds. But at least it's a start, and if for these reasons you have come to Jesus, welcome. Nevertheless, be prepared, for he is likely to call to you in the crowd, "Mary, Bill, Jim, Jane, follow me."

II

A second level of discipleship is that of those who came to Jesus not only to see and be seen, they came—and still come—*to hear* what he had to say.

Some came to hear out of curiosity. They had naturally inquisitive minds and, like the ancient Athenian philosophers of whom Paul spoke, were ready always to hear some new thing. Aware that truth never can be fully grasped, and that it must always be pursued, they kept their minds open to the new teachers and teachings.

Others came to be up on the latest thing around town. They wanted to be able to talk about the latest philosophy, the newest insight, the most recent discovery. Making the cocktail circuit, they wanted to

THREE LEVELS OF DISCIPLESHIP

be "in" with the sophisticated. I heard recently of a new subscription service which tells you the title, author, and main idea of popular books, enabling you to name-drop with erudition without ever having to read the book. You have to be careful, of course, not to let the conversation go very far on any one subject. Keep it moving. Some people came to Jesus, and still do, in an effort to keep up on in-group name-dropping.

Others came to Jesus because they were intellectually interested. They made it their business to add information to information, book to book, teaching to teaching, in a sincere effort to come to the truth. Jesus had become important enough so that the intellectuals had to reckon with him. They still do, and some come to him for that reason, and are, to a considerable degree, reasonably satisfied.

There were other people who came to listen to Jesus to see if they could get an endorsement of their own views. Convinced in their own minds of the rightness of their position, they came to Jesus not to receive, but to take; not to learn, but to use Jesus' prestige to support their own prejudice. Of itself, his teaching had little value to them, except as they could use it to support their preconceived notions. They saw Jesus as a power to be exploited.

In that respect, nineteen centuries of history have not changed the crowd much. Jesus has been used to endorse both capitalism and socialism. He has been

PUTTING YOUR LIFE ON THE LINE

asked to bless dictatorships and democracies. Both unions and management have claimed his alliance. During the sixties protests, old and young alike believed Jesus to be on their side of the conflict. Hawks and doves claimed him, as did anarchists and law-and-order advocates. Consequently, Jesus himself often got drowned out.

Are you at that second level of discipleship? Have you come out of curiosity and intellectual interest? Are you here to get endorsement of your own future plans, reinforcement of inadequate visions of the future, support for your favorite social scheme to end all our problems? Fine. At least that's a starting point. But be warned, for the Christ might call you out of the crowd to challenge you, to put your views to the test in the white-hot fires of history. It is one thing to hold a private opinion, but it is quite another to defend it publicly before a worldwide figure such as Jesus. Be prepared to be summoned to something beyond right thinking.

III

However, to be real followers of Jesus we must advance to the third level of discipleship—we must *act,* we must do what he says. "Why do you call me 'Lord, Lord,' and never do what I say?" Jesus asked in anguish. "I'm looking for people who *do* something, rather than just listen and talk. I'm looking for people who have the courage to act."

THREE LEVELS OF DISCIPLESHIP

We have many subtle ways of avoiding Christ's demands. We cherish our American freedoms—rightly so. Nevertheless, one of the strengths and weaknesses of our many freedoms is the opportunity to hear what we want to hear. Obviously, on the one hand, that is good. No one can feed us the party line. We can hear contrary views. But on the other hand, we often join groups which exclude the other views to promulgate only our own. Even in churches—sometimes especially in churches—we gather to hear only what we want to hear. Consequently, Jesus' command to act often falls on deaf ears.

Another problem people have is mistaking admiration for discipleship. It is one thing to admire Robin Graham for sailing around the world alone; it is quite another to follow after him. It is one thing to admire the astronauts, but quite another to sit on top that rocket ourselves. Many admire the tremendous accomplishments of our great musicians, but few want to put out the effort to follow in their steps.

Jesus is esteemed by many as a man of crystal character. They respect his teachings, especially the Sermon on the Mount, and they revere him as a good example, particularly for the young. Some think they might like to follow him, but not too closely. Others turn away when they hear his demands, for he wants them to act, to do.

And what does he want them to do? Go to the moon? Become a hockey star or a concert pianist or a

PUTTING YOUR LIFE ON THE LINE

worldwide adventurer? Thankfully no, for many of us could not do that even if we wished. Rather he asks of us two things possible for us all. Difficult, yes, but possible. At the third level of discipleship Jesus asks that we do the works of *believing* and *loving*. We do not have to be rich or powerful or wellborn to do that; nor do we have to be poor, weak, and on the wrong side of the tracks. Male or female, white or black, old or young—it makes no difference. Believing and loving are possible for us all.

And when we enter into the third level of discipleship of believing and loving, we experience very positive results. For one thing, doing what Christ asks takes us out of the smallness of ourselves, links us to a great leader and a great cause, stretching us to full stature. Tschaikowsky once said, "It is thanks to Mozart that I have devoted my life to music." What brought Indiana University back to the number one place in basketball? It was new coach Bobby Knight, who made severe demands and molded a balanced team, stretching them to their full stature.

Likewise, for centuries, Christ has been making giants out of pygmies. Timid men have been changed to stalwart soldiers of courage and fortitude. Self-centered, self-pitying, neurotic women have been transformed into radiant, outgoing, unselfish jewels of humankind. Young people defensively playing it cool, or frantically pursuing every sensual pleasure, have

THREE LEVELS OF DISCIPLESHIP

been brought to true joy and balanced self-identity by obedience to the Christ.

Recently at a public service I looked out into the congregation to see a radiant young college girl, attentive and receptive to the scripture and message. In a later conversation she told me that over one hundred fifty students in her dorm at Northern Michigan University gather for Bible study and prayer and singing. "It's just wonderful," she said, "what Christ has done for us." It really was. I could see it in her radiant countenance. What a difference from the drug, alcohol, and sex orgies prominent on so many campuses. Obedience to Christ transforms us from spiritual pygmies to spiritual giants.

The obedience of third-level discipleship also gives us a solid foundation for living. When Los Angeles had its rather severe earthquake recently, city residents found they had problems more difficult than broken bridges and crumbled buildings. They had psychological problems, especially with children, who no longer were sure of the earth. Justifiably, their faith in so-called terra firma was severely shaken.

When we come to the crisis and stress periods of life, will our foundations really hold up, or will they crumble and fall like those of Jesus' story? For example, if church and nation were built on the faith and values we hold, how firm would they be? Those things we hold most dear—are they worth passing on to others? What sort of communities would our beliefs

PUTTING YOUR LIFE ON THE LINE

and actions produce? Would they endure? Would they stand the tests of time, the grinding realities of history? Sincere followers of Christ have found him to be a man for all seasons, adequate for providing a firm foundation for all of life, producing a community of faith which has endured over nineteen hundred years.

A further reward of third-level discipleship is this: our knowledge of God increases. As Jesus once said: "Whoever has the will to do the will of God shall know whether my teaching comes from him or is merely my own" (John 7:17 NEB). John's first letter observes: "Here is the test by which we can make sure that we know him: do we keep his commands? The man who says, 'I know him,' while he disobeys his commands, is a liar and a stranger to the truth; but in the man who is obedient to his word, the divine love has indeed come to its perfection" (I John 2:3-5 NEB). F. W. Robertson, famous British preacher of the last century, said, "The condition of spiritual wisdom and certainty in truth is obedience to the will of God, surrender of private will."

Thus knowledge of God is not something confined to the intellectual or mystical elite. Instead, it is available to all in the doing of loving and believing.

Centuries ago when people were lamenting a lack of knowledge of God, the prophet Isaiah said, *"If* you will loose the fetters of injustice, *if* you set free those who have been crushed, *if* you share food with the hungry, *if* you give clothing and shelter to the needy; *then,"*

THREE LEVELS OF DISCIPLESHIP

says Isaiah, "God will answer, 'Here I am,' and he will be your guide and companion" (Isaiah 58). Those who *do* the acts of faith and love enter into the knowledge of God. They receive an inner assurance that God sees and cares and stands by them.

Albert Schweitzer, son of a German Lutheran pastor, brilliant, exceptionally talented, extraordinarily gifted, and well-educated, could have gone anywhere with any career of his choosing, be it medicine, philosophy, music, theology. In a sense, Europe was at his disposal. But then he says, "While at the university and enjoying the happiness of being able to study and even to produce some results in science and art, I could not help thinking continually of others who were denied that happiness by their material circumstances or their health. Then one brilliant summer morning at Gunsbach, during the Whitsuntide holidays—it was in 1896—there came to me as I awoke, the thought that I must give something in return for it." Subsequently, Schweitzer decided to become a medical missionary.

Amid all the advantages and opportunities we enjoy, do we not hear, with Albert Schweitzer, Jesus' call to a higher level of discipleship? Have we only been a part of the crowd, religious moochers and spectators? Are we now ready to take up our cross to follow him?

The High Cost of Loving
Mark 10:17-22

We talk a good deal about the high cost of living, and with good reason. It is costly to live. We know that, every time we buy the expensive new dress or suit which falls apart because of inferior thread and shoddy workmanship. Or when we take the kids to the shopping center for the new set of school clothes and shoes. Or when we prepare to enroll them in college and find that tuition, room, and board have taken yet another rise.

Old people feel it too, having saved to some degree for retirement, but never enough, it seems, to offset inflation. Automatic cost-of-living increases of 7 or 8 percent are commonplace in union contracts and salary negotiations, not to mention the floating

THE HIGH COST OF LOVING

cost-of-living clause in the current Social Security law. It costs more to live these days—a hard economic fact not to be unnoticed by those who want the church to live vigorously.

But let us consider something more basic than high living costs. Let us talk about the high cost of loving, for true loving is costly indeed—so costly, in fact, that very few people wish to invest in it. For all our talk about love and loving, very few people have it or do it. Oh yes, there is a great deal of playing around with people's bodies, and all that. And there is a lot of sentiment and nostalgia that masquerades for love, persuading that wistful memories and occasional tender feelings are the sum and substance of love.

However, when Christians begin to talk of love, they do not talk for long until they realize how serious love is, how threatening and risky. Yet they also know it to be exhilarating, fulfilling, and ecstatically satisfying once it is experienced. However, let me warn you once again that the way of love is a risky, perilous way. Love's gift of fulfillment is not easily attained. You will not find it at any bargain counter of flimsy commitments or at any discount store of easy sex.

Love is costly because it demands three difficult acts of the will or three payments, three acts of surrender: the surrender of our worship of aesthetics; the surrender of our worship of ethics; and finally the surrender of our worship of the self. The question is, of course, whether we are willing to pay such a high cost.

PUTTING YOUR LIFE ON THE LINE

I

Let us consider the first payment—*the surrender of our worship of the aesthetic.*

Sometimes in our more reflective moods, we are able to see through the hold which the aesthetic dimension has on us. Have you, like me, ridden along in the car or airplane, looking out on the beautiful landscape, wondering what it's all about? If you are like me, you are greatly impressed with the awesome mystery of the ocean and huge lakes, the dazzling majesty of the mountains, or the humble but amazing ornate beauty of the flowers. We do have a great aesthetic sense. No wonder many peoples in the history of religions have taken delight in the worship of some of nature's beautiful objects.

But frankly, for all nature does give us (and of course, it gives us a great deal—our air, water, and food) it does not in all its satisfactions fully satisfy. Inspiring as nature is, it is not quite inspiring enough. Sustain us though it does, something there is within us that looks elsewhere for a more complete sustenance. Speak all you will to an ocean surf, or shout all you will to the deep forest, or yodel as you like on the great mountain slopes, the only response you get is your own echo, or the whine of the wind through the trees or over the waves.

Mute as nature sometimes is, many people still hold on to the aesthetic dimension as the ultimate, finding God in the lake's vast expanse or the mountain's silent

THE HIGH COST OF LOVING

Christians have not been alone in their embrace of the ethical, moral dimension as the ultimate religious reality. Judaism has many times taken that stance. For example, there is in the Jewish Talmud a story of a certain rabbi who, when a hostile army was at the gates of his town, went up on to his rooftop with his Book of Law to pray. His prayer went like this: "Lord of the worlds, if I have failed to follow one single word of this book of the Law, so let them [the hostile army] come in; but if not, then let them depart." Our latest report indicated that upon completion of the prayer, the army stormed the city and has held control ever since! Subsequently, both Christians and Jews have been reluctant to make such prayers on rooftops!

But in the stages on life's way, it often is the natural thing to move from the aesthetic stage to the ethical. Disenchanted with things, the self becomes interested in people, thankfully enough. Bored with beautiful objects, the self seeks out persons who can reciprocate and respond more than nature or art. Dissatisfied with just the right atmosphere, the self now begins its search for just the right people.

As Americans, we have been in past years preoccupied with things. Many of us, raised during the Depression, had scarcity and poverty as the major threats with which we had to deal. Insecurity was the absence of things. No wonder then that we developed an overwhelming drive for the accumulation of goods. We wanted to be sure of our security against any

PUTTING YOUR LIFE ON THE LINE

future depressions. We saved a lot, invested in real estate, and made it a point to have plenty of food on hand in well-stocked freezers. Emotions were sublimated and their energies channeled into production of goods. Satisfaction and fulfillment were found in industrial growth rates. Progress was defined as increased power to make and manipulate things.

But in an age of affluence, we have been freed, to some degree at least, from our preoccupation with things. Now we can give attention to causes and people. The other person rather than the other thing has begun to capture our interest. In various sensitivity and encounter groups, in psychologically oriented plays and movies and novels, in the popular rise of sociology, we have explored more and more the fascinating world of persons.

And it has been a long awaited, much needed exploration. For what is life if it is not relationships with people? If one thinks back over his life to point to its high spots, people and relationships come immediately into focus. Enamored as we sometimes are with places and things, a careful look often shows that they have value because they have association with people and personal relationships. Thus, the church where you were married, the grave where your father was buried, the vase your mother loved so dearly—all these tend to take their real value from their association with people.

Consequently, the move in our own time of many of

THE HIGH COST OF LOVING

our young people from a thing-obsessed, production-oriented life-style is most welcome. We are centering in more closely on what life is all about. No wonder, then, our present-day interest in human rights and movements of righteous cause. Long overdue is our concern for the health and welfare of ourselves and our fellows in a non-polluted environment in place of our obsession with more and more growth, more and more production, more and more consumption of our natural resources. We have realized that infinite growth is not possible on a finite planet. But more important, we are realizing that as human beings, we are all in this together. And in our realization, we are caught up in human causes, ethical causes, causes for our brother man. And it is a marvelously new and rewarding thing—this ethical dimension—an important stage on life's way. It represents a great new movement of the human spirit. Many rejoice in it.

But now I am going to suggest what will seem to be the strangest and most preposterous thing—namely, that this dimension must be surrendered, given up. In the name of Jesus this dimension must die. Absurd, some of you will say. Unchristian, others will reply. Impossible, assert the humanitarians. After all, this dimension is what life is all about, says the Ethical Culture Society. What is more important, many will ask, than loving your fellowman? And I will reply, hardly anything is more important, save one thing—loving God.

PUTTING YOUR LIFE ON THE LINE

God, we are told by Jesus, is a very demanding lover. He will tolerate gladly other loves, but only when he is first. He will occupy no second-rate position. With him, it is all or nothing at all. Thus, to enter the kingdom of God, Jesus kept saying that it was necessary to put God before all possessions and things. More than that, the relationship with God was to take precedence over all others. Jesus asserted that to enter the kingdom of God, all other loving relationships had to take second place—even the love of family. That is why loving has such a high cost. When it comes to loving God, everything has to be put on the line.

III

This brings us then to the third and most difficult payment of all—*the payment of the self itself.* It is precisely here that most of us, like the rich young ruler of our scripture, turn away sorrowful, for that is the one thing we are most reluctant to give up. And strange as it may seem, I believe that is what Jesus was really after in his conversation with the rich young man. Jesus was not after his things or his money, for it was suggested he give all that to the poor. Nor was he after his ethical commitment. The rich young man already had demonstrated the high quality of his morals and ethics. He had kept the commandments from his youth up.

THE HIGH COST OF LOVING

What then did he lack? Not money, nor ethics. In fact, in keeping with the theology of the time, he believed his money and moral behavior made him highly qualified for the kingdom of God. Most of his contemporaries, when asked to point out a good, religious man, would most surely have pointed at him. He would have been, in their estimation, an exemplary citizen of the kingdom.

But Jesus, as usual, saw more deeply. He wanted to find out what the man really loved. Was it his moral standing and respectable reputation? Well, yes. Was it his things, his possessions, his money? Jesus asked. Well, yes. Was it God and the kingdom of God? Well, there must be some mistake.

There is no mistake, said Jesus. It is a very simple question, yet an extremely difficult one. Do you love God more than all your things and all your great, worthwhile causes? Are you willing to give them all up for God's kingdom?

Rich young man, says Jesus, you have even greater potential than you realize. I need you for the kingdom of God. But it is a question of loyalty, you know. We need men who really are committed, men who are willing to lose their very selves in commitment. Therefore, if you are agreeable to selling all that you possess and giving the proceeds to the poor, we would be glad to include you. We love you and need you. But we must have your primary loyalty. What do you say?

PUTTING YOUR LIFE ON THE LINE

Well, rich young men and women, well-off middle-aged Americans and older people too, what do we say? What do we love most of all, really? Things or God? Causes or God? Self or God?

In a recent article in the *Atlantic* entitled "The Last Days of Cowboy Capitalism," the author, "Adam Smith," maintains that Harvard Business School graduates and postgraduates are today willing to accept the corporation and its production-oriented, thing-producing goals. But beyond that, they are looking for something inner. They do not want a "dumbbell life," with work at one end and home life at the other with a freeway or commuter train connecting the two. They feel that work should fit life, and they are concerned about intimate relationships with their families, and so on.

Then "Adam Smith" quoted a former dean of admissions: "So if I had to divide the decades again, I would still say that the fifties produced the corporate man who would rise to the top and die seventeen months after retirement, leaving a beautiful estate; the sixties students wanted a piece of the action; and currently the fantasy is a balanced life—just *enough* success to include it all; they want to run things but not at any cost; they still want power but now they want love, too" (*Atlantic,* September 1972, p. 49).

That was the rich young man of our scripture. He wanted power, but he wanted love too. He wanted the best of both worlds. Could he have it? he asked Jesus.

44

THE HIGH COST OF LOVING

That remains to be seen, said Jesus. To have the best of the kingdom of God you have to lose your life, give up your self-righteous causes, sell your possessions, and come follow me.

You must be kidding. Come on, Jesus, you're putting me on. What are you, some kind of fanatic or something? It was a good joke, and all that, but now tell me, what do you really mean?

Sorry, rich young man, that's what I really mean. You're a big boy now, and you have great potential for God's kingdom. But you have to move out of your adolescent state of mind, out from behind your mother's fondling indulgence into the world of God's people. If the great leaders and commanders of the world ask the devoted allegiance of their followers, do you think God asks any less?

You say you want God's love, want to be a part of his kingdom, want to have a great share in his new adventure. Very well, sell everything. Give up your pride. Lose your life for my sake, and you will find it.

You know the story. The rich young man went away sorrowful. And many rich young men ever since have turned away sorrowful.

How about you? How about me? But do you know what I think? I think if the rich young man had said, "All right, I'll do that, I'll sell everything," Jesus then would have said, "Never mind. You don't need to now, because if I have you, I'll have all you own, too."

I ask you now to renew your vows to God, to die to

pride, to causes, to things, so that you might renew your primary allegiance to God. That is the high cost of loving. And once you do that, the ethical, aesthetic dimensions once again will come alive, but this time from a new perspective. The first great commandment is to love the Lord our God with all our heart, soul, mind, and strength. Then we are to love our neighbor as our self. And we shall find that loving costs a lot in these dimensions as well. It is the high cost of loving translated into dollars and intelligence and energy. And that is where our financial commitment to the church should show up. It is here that our willingness to pay the high costs of loving begins to manifest itself.

There is only one thing that costs more than loving, and that is hating. The cost is broken homes, runaway children, organized crime, debilitating addictions, violent relationships, and wars of bloodshed.

Churches are organized to pay the high cost of loving. And in this day, they need you greatly to help pay the bill. Is there any real alternative?

Jesus and the Deserters
Matthew 26:36-56

From its very beginning, the Christian faith, like many other great movements, has been plagued by deserters. Paul was deserted by young John Mark on one of their missionary journeys. Peter once deserted Paul at Antioch in his temporary lapse into conservative Judaistic Christianity. And on the night of the Last Supper, the disciples soon were to desert their leader and master, the man who had been the focus of their lives and dreams for three years of intense activity.

Jesus, extraordinarily sensitive and perceptive man that he was, seemed to sense the forthcoming crisis of faith for the disciples. Even while they were eating their last supper together, he said, "You will all fall away because of me this night; for it is written, 'I will strike

PUTTING YOUR LIFE ON THE LINE

the shepherd, and the sheep of the flock will be scattered'" (RSV). But Peter, robust and impetuous, objected, insisting that "though they all fall away because of you, I will never fall away. . . . Even if I must die with you, I will not deny you." And all the disciples said the same thing.

Oh Peter, such brave words, such great intention and high resolve. Sitting in the theater of history, we can see your bravado and the too easy acclamations of loyalty on the part of your fellow disciples. So very soon your fickleness and fear will be the talk of the centuries. Even though you stole away in the darkness of Gethsemane and Jerusalem, the searchlight of history has found you and exposed you to the scrutiny of the prophets and martyrs of the ages. What you did in secret has been proclaimed over the media of the world.

And yet Peter's story is too often our story, the disciples' fickleness our fickleness. For we know that when we finally come down out of the theater seats and ourselves get involved in the action of history, we too have our problems of loyalty to Jesus and his cause. Like Peter, we have done more than our share of denying our association with Jesus. We have been involved in betrayal and deceitfulness along with Judas. And when in the crucial hour demands have been made, we, like the disciples, too often have slipped off into the darkness to get lost in the crowd of history's onlookers.

JESUS AND THE DESERTERS

Nevertheless, we cannot help wondering, Why did the disciples desert him? Did they not know the importance of the moment? Were they not aware that the course of the world's history was about to be altered irrevocably? Could they not sense they were in the presence of the world's greatest man? Did they not realize that very night was the momentous launching of a communal meal which would be celebrated subsequently by millions upon millions of followers in almost every country and language, to say nothing of its being observed by a man on the moon? Could they not see that this, their leader whom they were deserting, would inspire more music, books, and poetry than any man in history?

And how about us? Why would we desert such a man? Do we suffer from the same problems as the original disciples? What are the causes of desertion? And what are their remedies?

I

No doubt one of the reasons the disciples ran was the *natural instinct of fear.* We have to keep in mind that the disciples were expecting to achieve a sweeping political victory with Jesus. They had become fully convinced he was God's own chosen candidate to bring in the revolutionary government which would re-establish Israel's independence and re-introduce her Golden Age. After all, they had just been through the exhilarating procession of palms, and their expections and excitement were running wild.

Therefore they were off guard late at night in the Garden of Gethsemane when the soldiers came with Judas for the arrest. Had they not just shared a tremendously significant meal together? Had not Jesus indicated that victory for their cause was near when he said he would not eat with them again until the new kingdom had come? They expected their next dinner party together would be a victory banquet soon after the impending revolution. Their thoughts were on the glory of triumph, the sweet fruits of success. They fully expected to share in the limelight of Jesus' ascendancy to the royal throne.

Consequently, they were completely flustered and confused that night in Gethsemane. Even when Jesus was wrestling with the question of whether or not to attempt violent revolution or to take his chances on God's action and intervention, the disciples were drowsy and sleepy. Feeling the effects of too much dinner wine, their spirit was willing but their flesh was weak. Thus they were ill prepared to cope properly with the enemy.

And although Peter drew his sword it was futile to resist. Jesus' thousands of supporters were bedded down for the night, unaware that their leader was being taken captive.

Thus out of instinctive fear, the disciples scattered. Jesus was captured. They would be next, and in the

JESUS AND THE DESERTERS

darkness and confusion they deserted. Everything was so unexpected, so unplanned, and they were so bewildered they knew only one thing to do—run.

We know that feeling. There are times when fear grips us and in our urge for survival we respond instinctively by getting out of there. It is natural and perhaps excusable, but it is desertion. We've been caught in situations like that, when we should have stood up to let ourselves be counted as Christ's own, but out of fear we beat it or we remained silent when we should have spoken out. Many times Jesus and his church have looked beseechingly at us for support and we have turned away, out of fear maybe. We might have saved the day, changed the course of things, but we stole away into the night of noncommitment and noninvolvement.

II

But there are other reasons why disciples desert. Perhaps one was *their intention to escape arrest* and then *to regroup to plan their aggressive strategy* for Jesus' release and their revolution. We would be both charitable and perhaps historically accurate to see that as part of their motivation for running. No need for them all to get arrested. Escape and counterattack would be much wiser and nobler.

I am sure many of us would agree. The disciples were loyal, but they were also trying to be shrewd political strategists. Nevertheless, it is precisely here the

PUTTING YOUR LIFE ON THE LINE

disciples were not keeping up with their leader. They were sleeping through the crucial moments of his agonizing Gethsemane prayer, and many of his earlier statements on suffering and nonviolence went over their heads.

Consequently, they were several steps behind Jesus, still not up with him on insight, still not perceiving the deep realities of history that he was seeing. Thus their temporary desertion seemed to say to Jesus that they knew better what was going on than he did, and that they would rescue him from the mess into which he had gotten himself.

We have done the same thing. We have done it in our colleges and universities. We have deserted Jesus for a different strategy because we think we know better how to bring in the kingdom of God. So we have built gigantic, assembly-line learning factories, shoving second- and third-rate teachers at our young people while the better minds concern themselves with publication and research. And many institutions of higher learning have thrown off any responsibility for teaching character, morals, or values; while at the same time some of our high schools are discovering our desparate need for precisely those things. One second-grade teacher is even devoting a section of class time and material to teaching manners.

How often do we desert Jesus and his church for better strategies for handling human affairs, as if we knew so much better what to do than he? Like the

JESUS AND THE DESERTERS

original disciples, we can almost hear ourselves call out in the darkness as he is being led away, "Don't worry, Jesus. We'll save you from your illusions. We'll save you from yourself. We'll handle it. We have a better strategy. We'll take care of things violently."

Some desert Jesus believing more in reason than in love, deluding themselves with the idea that if people simply *know* the good, they will *do* it, that all the problems of man are simply reducible to ignorance and not to hate or perverted will or to pride or selfishness. So we call out as we leave him alone, "Don't worry Jesus, we'll be back with our soldiers and professors to rescue you from your delusions." But he saw nineteen centuries ago what a few people are beginning to see today—namely, that our violent impulses and sophisticated weapons of destruction threaten the annihilation of the human race.

III

A third reason for the desertion of the disciples may have been *cowardice, a lack of willingness really to take a responsible stand, and to bear the fault and shame of possible failure.*

It is true that the disciples had suffered some abuse during the latter period of Jesus' ministry. When they had first started out, and when the movement was growing rapidly, gaining momentum and ascendancy, the disciples basked in favorable and sometimes wildly enthusiastic public acclaim. Perhaps there always are more heroes in the first flush of battle when hopes are high and expectations are unthwarted by death or defeat.

But as the campaign draws on, the men are separated from the boys. The starry-eyed recruits looking more for adventure and excitement than for a kingdom and a cause soon have second thoughts flooding their minds. Many people are courageous for the short burst of glory but cowardly for the long hard pull. When the battle draws on long and hard, it is easier to let George do it. Is that what the disciples said when they fled Gethsemane? "You stay with him, Peter, or you, John or James. You're the inner circle, after all, so you stick by him. We'll just be on our way, fast like." And young John Mark must have thought the same thing, for he was in the garden with only his bed sheet wrapped around him. And when the soldiers grabbed that, he ran off in a hurry to become the first streaker in the New Testament!

But we've done our share of streaking—streaking of a different kind, of course—streaking out of Christ's army, out of his cause. We see it in our contemporary cowardice with respect to morality, or should I say immorality. We lament the moral and ethical problems of today, but we will not take the responsibility for them. We admit we have problems, but claim no one is to blame. Courts repeatedly hand down "guilty" verdicts on the Watergate defendants, but everyone pleads innocent. Everything is corrupt, but no one has done anything wrong. The whole system is rotten, but

JESUS AND THE DESERTERS

there are no rotten apples. It's a dog-eat-dog world, but everyone believes he is the dog being eaten. No one is bad, no one is wrong, no one is at fault, no one has willed any evil. If any wrong has been done, it's always the other guy. I'm OK, you're OK; it's everyone else who is causing the trouble. So it's no-fault insurance, no-fault divorce, no-fault immorality, no-fault discipline problems. Everything is wrong, but no one is at fault.

Ah, such childishness, such deceitful buck-passing! Ours has been a century which prided itself as man-come-of-age, man-responsible-for-himself. Yet the truth is, we often have become a generation of moral cowards, unwilling to stand up to be counted for Christ's cause of right.

No doubt some of those early disciples thought they could beat it out of the Garden in the darkness and retreat to the lake in the north in Galilee to live out their days in peace and quiet, without the imminent risk of death. And we often are the same, are we not? Jesus calls us to take a stand for the right, and we duck out or pass the buck or say it's George's fault, or it's his responsibility. What we do not realize is that the course of history often is being changed in obscure gardens like Gethsemane while we are retreating into the bushes.

Thus in our land today, we have more than our share of deserters—people who, out of the instinct of natural fear and survival, vanish into the darkness.

PUTTING YOUR LIFE ON THE LINE

They have not yet mastered their animal instincts. Others desert because they believe they are better and wiser than the master. They believe Jesus would do better if they led him, rather than letting him lead them.

And then there are the moral and spiritual cowards—people who sometimes talk a big game, but who have not the fortitude to say, "It's me, it's me, O Lord, standing in the need of prayer." We have spiritual cowards who, when they are wrong, cannot say, "I am wrong, I have sinned." Instead they always say, "I confess George did it."

What the church needs, what this country needs, is people who will commit themselves anew to the Christ, saying, "Lord, count me in. I'm on your side—sign me up. I'm yours to the end." May God grant us that kind of faith and courage.

The Fool on the Hill
Matthew 27:41-42

Day after day alone on a hill
   the man with the foolish grin is
   keeping perfectly still,
But nobody wants to know him,
   they can see he's just a fool
   and he never gives an answer.

But the fool on the hill sees the sun going down and
the eyes in his head see the world spinning 'round.

Well on the way, head in a cloud,
   the man of a thousand voices talking perfectly
   loud,
But nobody ever hears him,
   or the sound he appears to make
   and he never seems to notice.

PUTTING YOUR LIFE ON THE LINE

> But the fool on the hill sees the sun going down and
> the eyes in his head see the world spinning 'round.

Whether Beatles John Lennon and Paul McCartney had Jesus in mind when they wrote that song, I do not know. But it is easy to see Jesus described in the song.

His contemporaries surely saw him as a fool. Not that he was an idiot or imbecile; rather his foolishness was in the apparent wrong use of his energies, the misapplication of his intelligence, his foolhardy devotion to a futile cause. He had been foolish enough to give himself to the idealism of the kingdom of God. What others talked about, dreamed about, and hoped for, Jesus attempted to actualize. The far-off divine event, which others held out as a combination carrot and pacifier, Jesus tried to grasp for the present day. His mistake was that of taking too seriously his dreams. His delusion was believing he could make real what others only talked about. He was the fool on the hill.

Herod Antipas, the Jewish puppet-king of Galilee, surely thought so. Though he saw Jesus as a threat, a possible leader of revolution, he at the same time had contempt for Jesus and his lack of strategy, his belief in nonviolence, and his unprotected entrance into Jerusalem. In Herod's eyes Jesus was foolish because he made himself so vulnerable. Pilate, the Roman governor of Judea, was in agreement with Herod.

THE FOOL ON THE HILL

Jesus was too naïve to be a real leader or king. As Jesus stood trial before Pilate and the mob shouted "Crucify him, crucify him," Pilate said (in the rock opera *Jesus Christ, Superstar*):

> "I see no reason—I find no evil
> This man is harmless so why does he upset you?
> He's just misguided—thinks he's important
> But to keep you vultures happy I shall flog him."

But the mob is unsatisfied and shouts again,

> "Crucify him, crucify him."

Pilate then turns to Jesus, asking:

> "Where are you from Jesus? What do you want Jesus? Tell me.
> You've got to be careful—you could be dead soon—could well be.
> Why do you not speak when I have your life in my hands?
> How can you stay quiet? I don't believe you understand."

Jesus replies:

> "You have nothing in your hands
> Any power you have comes to you from far beyond."

Then Pilate erupts in contempt:

> "You're a fool Jesus Christ—how can I help you?
> Don't let me stop your great self-destruction.

PUTTING YOUR LIFE ON THE LINE

> Die if you want to you misguided martyr.
> I wash my hands of your demolition,
> Die if you want to you innocent puppet!"

And so Pilate and Herod and the Sanhedrin and the mob put a fool on the hill, a would-be king with a martyr complex, a naïve country bumpkin from the unsophisticated hill country of the north. Or so they thought. And so we think sometimes.

And yet, that fool on the hill has attracted our attention for over nineteen centuries. Some of the world's most beautiful music and poetry has been written about him. Millions gather weekly all over the world to worship in his name. All of Western civilization has been profoundly influenced by this fool, whereas Herod and Pilate are mentioned only incidentally in relation to the story of the fool.

What, then, is the mysterious power of the fool on the hill? Is Jesus actually wiser than Herod or Pilate? Why do we honor the fool? And why does he look so foolish?

I

In the first place *Jesus looked foolish because he took a chance on the new.*

In some societies the new has been regarded as an enemy, an intruder into the established order of things. As traditions, habits, and customs were passed down from generation to generation, they soon became elevated to a near heavenly status. Even habits of

THE FOOL ON THE HILL

thought became rigid and fixed, established in stone hearts and inflexible minds. The novel and new might be dreamed about in theory, but in practice it was to be resisted. "The earth is the center of the solar system" or "the earth most certainly is flat" or "if man was meant to fly the good Lord would have given him wings" or "man will never make it to the moon because God didn't intend that he should explore space"—truisms such as these were a part of a rigid past.

Thankfully, however, we have had people who were willing to take a chance on the new. And plenty of them made fools of themselves, crashing to the ground after having taken off from the barn roof in a pair of homemade wings, or making imprecise statements about the universe after looking through the first telescopes, or having multi-million-dollar rocket programs that failed. Nevertheless, some people took a chance on a new dream, risked themselves on a vision, and launched out into the future in faith and hope. Let all so-called hardheaded realists and traditionalists remember that if the future had been left up to them we would still be riding horses and only looking enviously at birds, not imitating them. The nineteenth and twentieth centuries have been characterized by so-called fools who took a chance and introduced the industrial, technological revolution.

Much the same can be said for medicine. Our modern hospitals and clinics are light years away from

PUTTING YOUR LIFE ON THE LINE

the primitive medical theories and treatments of just a few short years ago. Brave men launched out into the unknown to make it known, to chart new pathways through the seas of ignorance, to risk themselves in the uncertainty of the new, thus revolutionizing medicine. Many of us today are alive because of these men, these foolish men who dared to dream and to stake their lives on their visions. Some people called them fools, but now we call them heroes—heroes because they have led mankind to new levels of reality never thought possible by lesser minds.

Likewise with Jesus and human society. He was convinced mankind did not have to live impaled on old fears, constricted by old grudges, and circumscribed by myopia. He had a vision of a new society where people would not pigeonhole their neighbors, but help them develop and grow. He saw a realm where the humble in spirit, rather than the arrogant, would be called children of God. He envisioned an existence where the pure in heart would see God and the meek would inherit the earth.

Jesus had grown tired of the old rules for living—an eye for eye, tooth for tooth, hate your enemies, curse those that curse you. He was weary of the law of the social jungle, where the meanest and cruelest and most brutal survived. He was tired of the superiority of the arm that swings the sword over the arm that plays the harp. Jesus repudiated the vile cursing and words of threat and death breathed out of the mouths of the

THE FOOL ON THE HILL

world's violent men, and upheld instead the poetic visions of Isaiah, the profound prayers of the psalmists, the earnest aspirations of men of peace. He was weary of kingdoms being built again and again on revenge and spilled blood, and he taught and preached unceasingly of a kingdom built on repentance, openness, mutual help, free development, and blood willed for the good.

Sitting in the pomp and splendor of imperial but brutal Rome, Pilate scoffed at Jesus, as did Herod, sitting in the shadow power of his shadow kingdom. But even more regrettably, we often have found ourselves sitting beside Pilate and Herod, rather than standing beside Jesus. Even yet, after nineteen centuries, we find ourselves thinking the kingdoms of Pilate and Herod to be more real than Jesus' kingdom. The ironic thing is that even though Jesus lived long ago, and was killed as a man who was ahead of his time, we kill him over and over again as a man ahead of our time.

But think again. Both Pilate and Herod are remembered only because they are dragged along on the coattails of Jesus' reputation. Their kingdoms long since have fallen and faded, whereas the kingdom of God, of which Jesus spoke, goes on from strength to strength, coming alive in each generation, circling the earth and jumping to the moon with its new realities, its joy of loving and forgiving in place of hating and avenging.

PUTTING YOUR LIFE ON THE LINE

Who now can remember the people who laughed at Galileo and scorned Copernicus? Who now can name the detractors of the Wright brothers and Thomas Edison? Who can remember the scoffers of Louis Pasteur, the ridiculers of Isaac Newton? Fools in their own day, they are heroes in ours because they took a chance on the new.

Likewise with Jesus. Likewise with his church. The future becomes a reality with those who are willing to take a chance on the new. Someone has quipped that the seven last words of the church are: We've never done it that way before. The ironic thing is that the way out of death, the way out of bondage to the past, often is the way of the fool, the way of risk, of taking a chance on the new.

II

In the second place, *Jesus looked foolish because he took a chance on love.*

Almost all of us have some kind of idea of that kind of foolishness. Robert Goulet sings the popular song "What Kind of Fool Am I?" and we know what he means. When we fall in love, we extend ourselves, open ourselves up, make ourselves vulnerable, and thus easily make fools of ourselves, because we lose our cool. Other popular singers resolve, "I'll never fall in love again." Why? Well, for one thing, when you kiss you can get enough germs to kill you. But the real reason is that we can be killed with a broken heart,

THE FOOL ON THE HILL

crushed by a lover who forsakes us. When we take a chance on love, we take a chance on being hurt. As preacher-poet John Donne said long ago:

> I am two fools, I know,
> For loving, and for saying so
> In whining poetry.

Many of us in our time have grown accustomed to ridiculing the medieval period of European history as a time of darkness, ignorance, and superstition. Rival kingdoms, fortified behind their huge fortresses, dotted the landscapes. Their inhabitants ventured forth only when they were sure they would not encounter the enemy.

If we could draw pictures of our psychological lives they would, in many ways, resemble life in a medieval fortress. Many people hide behind the walls of their castle, rarely venturing forth to encounter a friend, let alone a supposed enemy. Instead, they build a deep moat, erect high walls, and pull up the drawbridge to the heart of their lives. They do their living behind the high walls of security.

But any outside observer can see that it is a false security. Without exposure to and encounter with other people, they withdraw more and more into a suffocating self-embrace. Enclosed as they are, and walled about by the limitations of their own selves, they begin to die through atrophy, like the ancient dinosaurs. Restricted by their own self-imposed boun-

PUTTING YOUR LIFE ON THE LINE

daries they become spiritual pygmies and moral midgets. Ironically, their fortress becomes their prison. In the interest of preserving life, they have hastened death. Intending to preserve their freedom, they lose it. Wishing to free themselves from fear, they discover that fear has enslaved their freedom.

Not so with the fool on the hill. He took a chance on love, left his psychological fortress, and went out to encounter not only his friends but his enemies. Jesus walked out of the castle of self-righteousness into the open fields of life to breathe fragrances and to celebrate the vitality he found there. It would not do for him to ensconce himself behind his defenses, making himself impregnable, invulnerable. Love called him out to love, to give, to share, to act, and to be acted upon. Love drew him out for participation, for involvement, and yes, for suffering. Love made a fool of Jesus.

Or did it? Is hating wiser than loving? Is it smarter to be apathetic, cool, and indifferent than to be full of care and concern? Is it more real to tear down life or to build it up? To maim or to heal? To take life on the battlefield, or to give life in the surgical suite? To hoard life and goods and talent like Silas Marner, or to give life and goods and talent like Albert Schweitzer? "If only fools are kind, Alfie, then I guess it is wise to be cruel."

O Jesus, you fool on the hill, didn't you know? How could you be so naïve, so dumb, so stupid, so weak?

THE FOOL ON THE HILL

Why couldn't you have crushed your oppressors, slaughtered your enemies, recovered your losses, and established your kingdom in power? Oh Jesus, Jesus, you misguided martyr, why did you make such a fool of yourself?

And on the spring winds we hear a voice gently wafting its way down through the corridors of history, in and out of every land and heart, and the voice says, "I did it for God. I did it for you. I did it for love's sake."

> O where are kings and empires now,
> Of old that went and came?
> But, Lord, thy Church is praying yet,
> A thousand years the same.

The kingdoms of Cyrus and Ozymandias lie half-buried in the Near Eastern sands. Alexander the Great and Cleopatra are objects of history, but hardly of worship. Napoleon and Hitler and Stalin fade into the multicolored tapestry of mankind, but the kingdom of Jesus "is praying yet, a thousand years the same." And all because of the fool on the hill who took a chance on love.

III

In the third place, *Jesus looked foolish because he took a chance on death.*

In some ways this is the other side of taking a chance on love, because in so doing, we make ourselves open and vulnerable, susceptible to attack. As psychoanalyst Rollo May puts it, "To love completely carries with it the threat of the annihilation of everything. This intensity of consciousness has something in common with the ecstasy of the mystic in his union with God: just as he can never be *sure* God is there, so love carries us to that intensity of consciousness in which we no longer have any guarantee of security" (*Love and Will*, p. 101).

On the positive side, when we leave our medieval psychological fortresses we anticipate the fulfillment and ecstasy of love. But on the negative side, we know we also face the threat of death. It is here we see the irony of the so-called big brave men of the world who strut about in arrogance with a great show of bravado. They may be in fact masquerading, covering over their intense fear of death.

There is considerable reason to believe that our whole culture is caught up in this gigantic masquerade, this self-deception regarding death. We disguise the harsh reality of death and ignore the pangs of separation. Grief is repressed, and a happy demeanor is required. We satiate ourselves with drugs and alcohol, participate in the frantic search for pleasure, and strenuously avoid unpleasantries which have about them the suggestion of death.

But to love means to suffer. To grow means change and the threat of annihilation. To fly the first airplane, take the first serum, or suggest a new social order often

THE FOOL ON THE HILL

carries with it not only the threat of death, but its reality.

It is plain to see, therefore, that Jesus' way is not the way of cowards. His way separates the men from the boys. For when we take this chance on love, we take at the same time the chance on death. As Dr. May puts it, "When we love, we give up the center of ourselves. We are thrown from our previous state of existence into a void; and though we hope to attain a new world, a new existence, we can never be sure" *(ibid)*.

Likewise with Jesus. As viewed from behind all the fortresses of men, from behind Herod's castle and Pilate's palace, as seen from behind the entrenched powers and vested interests of the day, Jesus was a pathetic sight—a would-be king with a regal crown of thorns, a weed for a scepter, and a cross for a throne. He was the fool on the hill, the fool par excellence.

Or was he?

> Day after day alone on a hill
>   the man with the foolish grin is
>   keeping perfectly still.
> He never listens to them,
>   he knows that they're the fools,
>   they don't like him.
> But the fool on the hill sees the sun going down, and
> the eyes in his head see the world spinning 'round.

The Problem of Authority in Religion
Matthew 21:1-27

Approximately two thousand years ago Jesus rode into Jerusalem in his so-called triumphal entry. It was the Passover season, highest of all the Jewish religious festivals, and pious pilgrims were descending upon the city like hordes of locusts. Excitement naturally ran high but even more so this year, for it was rumored that Jesus the prophet would appear.

Although Jesus had been to Jerusalem before, he had concentrated his ministry more in the north, in Galilee. But at Passover time, everyone who could went down south to Jerusalem. Consequently, thousands of Jesus' most ardent northern, Galilean

THE PROBLEM OF AUTHORITY IN RELIGION

followers would be in the city along with thousands more supporters and sympathizers from the south.

It was not surprising, therefore, that the thronging pilgrims should erupt in cheers as Jesus made his way into the crowded, turbulent city. What had been hoped secretly for some time was now breaking out into the open—namely, that Jesus might be the great liberator, the Messiah, the King and Savior of Israel. Quite naturally Jesus' supporters burst into exuberant praise as they saw him coming. Messianic slogans were shouted: "Hosanna in the highest. Hosanna to the Son of David. Blessed is he who comes in the name of the Lord." Palm branches were laid in his path as a symbolic gesture of tribute. Some people even spread their cloaks on the road so that their triumphant King might enter the city on their own kind of red carpet.

Thus one of the great issues at stake was that of authority. By what authority does this man hold a parade without a permit? By what authority does he raise such a commotion? What right has he to incite revolution? By what authority does he throw the money-changers out of the temple, thus striking a blow at their lucrative enterprise?

The great issue was that of authority. No wonder the political and religious leaders were asking him where he got his. If he was not stopped, it was clear their own authority might be replaced with his.

Let me suggest that, two thousand years later, the issue is still essentially the same—it is the question of

PUTTING YOUR LIFE ON THE LINE

authority. Where *does* Jesus get his authority? But even more important for us, where do we get ours? Where do we find our authority for living, our authority for our morals and religion, for our philosophies and values? Where did Jesus find his? And why was he able successfully to challenge the established authorities of his own time? And can he challenge the established authorities of our time?

I

We note first of all that *Jesus had authority because he had overcome his fear of the people.*

Many of the religious officials of Jesus' time were, by contrast, afraid of the people. The Pharisees had separated themselves from the common people and consequently no longer understood them. For years they had paraded themselves as the only true religious people, the authentic examples of piety and godliness. By their super-pious professionalism they had excluded the populace.

But in the process they had lost their religious center. Consequently they hid behind the outward accoutrements of religious authority while lacking the deep, inward experiences and convictions out of which true authority comes. They were afraid the populace might find out that their pretentious religious system really was hollow, like Washington bureaucrats who fear the American people will discover the

72

THE PROBLEM OF AUTHORITY IN RELIGION

obsoleteness and irrelevance of their expensive, paper-shuffling bureaucracy.

But now the Pharisees' house of cards was beginning to tremble and shake. The common people heard Jesus gladly. Speaking to them with vigorous authority, he inspired crowds to gather around him. Unofficial, unlicensed, without proper credentials or background, Jesus became nevertheless their religious spokesman.

So when the Pharisees challenged Jesus, he countered with a challenge. What did they think of John the Baptist, whom the people regarded as God's prophet? Had they dealt openly, honestly, and humbly with the people, they would have been able to answer Jesus' question. But since they were not facing up to the real issue of genuine authority, since they really did not care about the people, since they were not really existentially involved, they could not answer Jesus. They were afraid of the people, afraid they would be exposed as the phonies they really were.

We have the same problem with religious authority. We are afraid of the people. We are afraid someone will discover how empty and hollow and pretentious our lives have been. We are afraid people will discover that we have been escaping the reality of the present moment by retreating to the past to hide behind mother's faith or father's reputation. We want to cloak ourselves with traditions and pedigrees, credentials and degrees, so that we will not have to face the reality of the now, our condition in the now. When we are asked if we love God or if we are followers of Christ, we give an evasive answer: "My grandfather was a minister" or "When I was young I was very religious."

The problem with authority in religion is our fear of people—fear of what our friends will say, fear of the sophisticated set which manages to conjure up yet another question, fear of whether they will accept us if we begin to live as though we had answers—adequate, authoritative, religious answers. We are afraid of what our peers will think, that they will accuse us of being too religious, fanatical even; afraid they will not invite us to their parties anymore, fearing that real religion turns one into a spoilsport; afraid we will not be a part of the in-group any more; afraid we will not be able to enjoy life if we take Jesus seriously—afraid, afraid, afraid. We, like the Pharisees, cannot answer Jesus' question of authority because we are afraid of people, because they and their opinions have so much authority over us. Jesus is challenging their authority—and he can do it because he himself is not afraid.

II

Furthermore, *Jesus had authority because he had overcome his fear of God.* On the one hand, people fear God has passed them by; but on the other hand, they fear God may get too close.

The Pharisees could not answer Jesus' question of

THE PROBLEM OF AUTHORITY IN RELIGION

authority because in their hearts they were afraid God had passed them by. Remember, they were the official representatives of God, the spokesmen for religion and morals. And yet John the Baptist, unofficial and without credentials, seemed to have the power of God working in him. Everyone was going to hear him, even King Herod.

Then Jesus appeared on the scene, and the crowds flocked to him. He too spoke with authority. While the Pharisees had the impeccable lineage, right connections, certificates and degrees, awards and honors, vestments and libraries, intimate knowledge of liturgy and ecclesiastical politics—while they had all that, they did not have authority; and hence they did not have the crowds—because they were afraid of God. They were afraid God had passed them by, had stood them up like a bride on wedding day.

And yet they had not really faced up to themselves or God. They had not owned up to the truth about themselves, because they were afraid of it. Psychologists and psychoanalysts know that phenomenon. Often they work for years with people who keep running from themselves and God, blaming parents and environment for their problems, constantly hiding behind one excuse or another, refusing to be responsible, unwilling to stand up like adults and be counted.

Likewise in religion. One intent of the message of God is to smoke a man out into the open, to challenge his self-deceit and self-righteousness, to put the searchlight on him, to press the question like the prosecuting attorney, asking, What do you think? What is the true reality—your system or God, your corporation or God, your organization or God?

To university presidents and faculty he asks, Are you concerned more with the truth or with political power, the physical plant, the size of your institution? To hospitals and medical people he points the finger and asks, Are you concerned with your gadgetry, your comfort and convenience, your own fulfillment and profit and reputation, or with the healing of people? Businessmen are asked about genuine quality and good service. Lawyers are questioned about justice and truth. Politicians are quizzed about integrity and credibility. Religious leaders are queried about authenticity, honesty, and genuine service to others. And with every question, men are tempted to hide behind their institutions, their traditions, their reputations, their families, their credentials.

Like the Pharisee who went up to the temple to pray, they thank God that they are not like other men, that they tithe, give alms, fast, pray, and do all the right things. But that kind of praying is beside the point, says Jesus. Imagine that—trying to impress God with their goodness, when they should say, "We are but unprofitable servants who have only done our duty." But we are afraid of God, afraid of him as we are of the psychoanalyst. We do not want him to look too deep

THE PROBLEM OF AUTHORITY IN RELIGION

or to probe around too much. We are afraid of what he will find, afraid we shall be found out for what we really are—namely, unfaithful lovers with fickle loyalties.

We are afraid of God because we fear he will discover that he is not the real authority in our lives, just as we are afraid our wives or husbands will find out we really do not love them. So we put God off, buy him guilt gifts, sing loudly, pray ostentatiously, give to charity—all good things by themselves, but sometimes we do them to put a smoke screen between ourselves and God. We do not want God to get too close. We are afraid of power. We like things we can control. We do not want anything to get out of hand—which is to say, out of *our* hands. That is often why churches are dead, institutions dull and powerless, and life boring and drab.

But Jesus faced up to himself and God. He stopped running, turned around, and dealt with the important, searching questions of life. Jesus finally said, OK God, I'm at your disposal; use me as you wish.

III

In the third place, *Jesus had authority because he was not afraid to put his life on the line.*

At the end of Jesus' famous Sermon on the Mount, Matthew says that the crowds "were astonished at his teaching, for he taught them as one who had authority, and not as their scribes" (7:28-29 RSV). In

PUTTING YOUR LIFE ON THE LINE

Jesus' case, as with any great teacher or leader, the problem of authority was implicit in his whole ministry almost from the beginning. People always were asking him for his credentials. Did he have degrees from the proper seminaries? Had he grown up in the best town and neighborhood? Was his family a member of the Palestinian Social Register? The answer was no—on all three counts. He had no letters of recommendation from recognized authorities. And even his hometown people questioned his right to speak out. They took such offense at him they even tried to kill him. Imagine that—his own neighbors threatening to do away with his life.

A lot has been said in recent years about the originality and authority of Jesus. Jewish scholars like Joseph Klausner have said that Jesus was "wholly explainable by the scriptural and Pharisaic Judaism of his time." There is nothing new in Jesus that cannot be found in the Talmud and other Jewish writings of the time, they said. But if that is the case, we must ask, why then do we not hear about the other teachers and scribes instead of Jesus? Why is it they have not changed the world instead of Jesus? Trying to explain Jesus away by the literary sources of the time is like trying to explain Abraham Lincoln away by noting the sources of his life and thought in nineteenth-century political science and religious literature.

The huge difference between Lincoln and his contemporaries is Lincoln himself. The huge dif-

THE PROBLEM OF AUTHORITY IN RELIGION

ference between Jesus and his contemporaries is Jesus. He taught with authority. He internalized the teaching, took his stand with it, identified his own life and person with it.

By contrast, the scribes were bookish and aloof, distant and reserved in their teaching. They presumed the answer to the latest religious question could be found in a book. Give them time to search it out and they would find it. Consequently, they never internalized the question of authority, they externalized it. They pushed it out onto someone else so that they themselves would not have to be responsible for the answer. Their approach to religion was roughly equivalent to that of a man who marries a woman largely on the recommendation of his friends. He is afraid to take his own stand, to make his own commitment, his own decision.

Thus, many teachers of Jesus' day were bookish, distant, reserved, aloof, dogmatic answer-men who never entered the situation existentially themselves. That is a problem not only of Jesus' time, but of ours. In the nineteenth century, theologian and philosopher Sören Kierkegaard chided the professors who always were running to their books for answers which ultimately could come only from themselves. And present-day theologian Frederick Herzog claims we do the same thing. Noting how the Protestant world always awaits the latest startling book to save us from our dilemmas, he laments, "There you have the

PUTTING YOUR LIFE ON THE LINE

genius of Protestantism: it's a book-religion. We're not saved by works, but by words-in-print."

Consequently the authenticity and ring of authority have vanished from our religion partly because of our book obsession, partly because of our unwillingness to take a subjective, existential stand on the issue of faith in God. Imagine our opinion of a man who, when asked if he loves his wife, says, Just a minute and I'll go ask my psychiatrist, or, Wait a moment until I have studied the matter longer. The authority and authenticity have gone out of that man, for he has objectified what, in the last analysis, can only be subjective. Authority and authenticity will return to that man only when he can say, Yes, I love my wife.

Do you love God? Do you love Jesus? Hard questions. And while ministers, theologians, philosophers, and others can help clarify what the question means, in the last analysis only you can respond. Yes, I love God. Yes, I love Jesus. That kind of answer cannot be found in any book. It can be found only within you, within your mind and heart; within me, within my mind and heart.

Thus Jesus taught with authority because he internalized his love of God. Consequently he either minimized or repudiated nonessential religious traditions. He emphasized the importance of right motives—motives such as love and service—over compulsive attention to religious trivialities. The individual and his conscience were elevated to great

THE PROBLEM OF AUTHORITY IN RELIGION

heights in Jesus' teaching. Each person is valuable in God's sight; the hairs of your head are numbered. No sparrow falls from heaven but he notices; therefore will he not much more care for you, O you of little faith? Thus Jesus took his courageous stand, backing his own teachings with the authority of his life. "It has been said to you of old, but *I* say unto you." This was his method. Unlike today's professor who quotes ad infinitum what other people believe, but who himself never takes a stand with his own belief, Jesus staked his life on the truth of his message. Consequently, he taught not as the scribes and Pharisees, but as one having authority—personal, existential authority.

Thus, after two thousand years, Jesus comes riding into town again on the words of five hundred preachers and a thousand choirs. We wave our palm branches, shout our hosannas, acclaim the coming of the king.

And two thousand years later, the essential questions are still the same. What is the authority for your life? To whom do you give your ultimate allegiance? What really claims your loyalty?

Are you wondering, like those crowds of long ago, whether or not Jesus really is an adequate king? Are you quizzical as to whether or not he is a sufficient authority, a capable enough leader? Is he sufficient to grapple with our anxieties and fears?

For the answer, we should now pull aside the curtain of history to see the great cloud of witnesses,

PUTTING YOUR LIFE ON THE LINE

that endless line of splendor, to hear them shout, "Yes, he is adequate; yes, he is sufficient; yes, he is indeed the king, and we love him, we love him." And the chorus swells with the Martin Luthers and Martin Luther Kings, the Peters and Pauls, the Puritans and Pilgrims, the teachers and preachers of the centuries; the Zwinglis and Calvins, the Savonarolas and Chrysostoms, the Fosdicks and Moodys, and saints like Anselm, Francis, and Aquinas. They all cry out, "Yes, yes, he is the king. He is the true authority. His perfect love has cast out all fear." Thus we say with Albert Schweitzer:

> He comes to us as One unknown, without a name, as of old, by the lake-side, He came to those men who knew Him not. He speaks to us the same word: "Follow thou me!" and sets us to the tasks which He has to fulfil for our time. He commands. And to those who obey Him, whether they be wise or simple, He will reveal Himself in the toils, the conflicts, the sufferings which they shall pass through in His fellowship, and, as an ineffable mystery, they shall learn in their own experience Who He is. *(The Quest for the Historical Jesus* [New York: Macmillan, 1968], p. 403)

The Message of Death
vs.
the Gospel of Life
Revelation 1:17-18; 21:5

Impossible, you say, that man survives
The grave—that there are other lives?
More strange, O friend, that we should ever rise
Out of the dark to walk below these skies.
Once having risen into life and light,
We need not wonder at our deathless flight.

Be brave, O heart, be brave:
It is not strange that man survives the grave:
'Twould be a stranger thing were he destroyed
Than that he ever vaulted from the void.

PUTTING YOUR LIFE ON THE LINE

Thus poet Edwin Markham spoke to his New York contemporaries earlier in this century, and thus he would speak to us today.

But we have come quite a distance since the thirties, and we are not so sure belief is as possible as Markham suggests. Perhaps our tendency toward the analytic, scientific mind has produced a certain melancholy of disbelief within us. Philosopher John Stuart Mill experienced that, a wearing away of his feelings by constant analysis. He recovered his joy of life in the discovery of poetry, by reawakening to a whole dimension of the world he had neglected.

Perhaps others of us have just been too busy to reflect upon the meaning of our lives, too active to consider their eternal significance. Many of us may be like the friend of drama critic Walter Kerr who, in a conversation, expressed two fears. "One was that if he did not slow down, he would have a heart attack. The other was that if he did not hurry up, he would not be able to accomplish enough that was useful before he had his heart attack."

Or maybe we have become too crass, too gross, too satiated and bland, blasé and hollow. As T. S. Eliot says, perhaps

> We are the hollow men
> We are the stuffed men
> Leaning together
> Headpiece filled with straw. Alas!
> Our dried voices, when

THE MESSAGE OF DEATH VS. THE GOSPEL OF LIFE

> We whisper together
> Are quiet and meaningless
> As wind in dry grass
> Or rats' feet over broken glass
> In our dry cellar

Even though we may be melancholy or super-busy or hollow, we are, nevertheless, believers of sorts. We are determined once again to consider the tenableness of the Easter faith. For some the faith is easy; for others, much more difficult.

But whatever the case, let me suggest that there really are only two alternative belief systems to consider. One system is the belief that death is the final end of everything. The other is the belief that life is victorious in the universe.

Let us consider then the message of death versus the gospel of life.

I

In the first place I believe *the natural world itself is on the side of life*.

One of the most basic philosophic questions of history is, Why is there something and not nothing? And a second important question is close behind, Why is there life and not non-life?

In answer to the first question, we posit God, who is not just a person, but Being-Itself—intelligent, loving being—out of which the world and life have come. We believe he has willed the world into existence, and that the impulse of life, with its immense complexity and order, comes from his mind and spirit.

The other classic explanation is much less satisfactory—the explanation which says that life and intelligence just happened to develop by chance over long periods of time. This violates our normal reasoning process, which suggests the lower cannot produce the higher. Wherever we see the inventions of man in the world we presuppose that the intelligence of man has been at work. Thus when we see the handiwork of nature, we presuppose the action of a higher intelligence we call God.

Therefore nature herself testifies to the power of life over death by the very fact of life itself, by the fact that inanimate minerals, combined with water and light, produce something higher, infinite in complexity and variety. Moreover, life keeps on reproducing itself. Though flowers die, their glory and life are passed on in their seed. And of course, animals and men pass on their life in the same way. That life should appear at all is a miracle. Therefore it should not be unbelievable that the same intelligence and power which started it could continue it.

Indeed, anthropologist and naturalist Loren Eiseley has written, "I am sure now that life is not what it is purported to be and that nature, in the canny words of a Scotch theologue, 'is not as natural as it looks'" *(The Immense Journey* [New York: Random House, 1957],

p. 197). It is not as easy to say as once we did, says Eiseley, that life arose "naturally" out of matter. "Once more, therefore, we are forced to examine our remaining notion that life is not coterminous with matter, but has arisen from it" *(ibid.,* p. 201).

Then Eiseley concludes his examination of "the immense journey" of life by stating, "I would say that if 'dead' matter has reared up this curious landscape of fiddling crickets, song sparrows, and wondering men, it must be plain even to the most devoted materialist that the matter of which he speaks contains amazing, if not dreadful powers, and may not impossibly be, as Hardy has suggested, 'but one mask of many worn by the Great Face behind'" *(ibid.,* p. 210).

Thus we would maintain the natural world itself is powerfully on the side of life.

II

However, more importantly, *we believe in the gospel of life* because of *its power to change people, to resurrect them again,* and to *bring civilizations alive.*

One of the most powerful facts supporting the Resurrection is the change in Jesus' disciples. What else could explain their metamorphosis from defeated, fearful men cowering in dread of death, to vigorous, courageous proclaimers of Christ's victory over the grave? After all, the real miracle in the world is a changed life. And something happened to make those disciples and the disciples of the ages into new men.

PUTTING YOUR LIFE ON THE LINE

Men may succeed in changing the face of the earth, but there is nothing so marvelous as a changed mind.

One of the great joys of the ministry is to see regularly the resurrection of people from old dead ways to vital new relationships and life-styles. The gospel of life has the power to make people into a new creation.

Nevertheless, the message of death abounds in every age, and in our twentieth century it often takes the form of meaninglessness, nihilism, and despair. As theologian Paul Tillich observed, "The decisive event which underlies the search for meaning and the despair of it in the 20th century is the loss of God in the 19th century. Feuerbach explained God away in terms of the infinite desire of the human heart; Marx explained him away in terms of an ideological attempt to rise above the given reality; Nietzsche as a weakening of the will to live. The result is the pronouncement 'God is dead,' and with him the whole system of values and meanings in which one lived" *(The Courage to Be* [New Haven: Yale University Press, 1952], p. 142).

So when God is dead, men have nowhere to turn but to themselves or to nature, the only other sources of life. Thus we have in our time a revival of classical romanticism and witchcraft and nature worship. Or in the hard lifelessness of our steel and glass canyons, we turn to the powers of sex. Like the followers of ancient fertility cults, we pray to our playmates and beauty

THE MESSAGE OF DEATH VS. THE GOSPEL OF LIFE

queens for vitality, for fulfillment and satisfaction, for reassurance that we are not nothing, but something.

When God is dead we become anxious about our identity, our self-worth, our immortality, because we do have an infinite longing within our breasts. As Wordsworth said,

> Our souls have sight of that immortal sea
> Which brought us hither,
> Can in a moment travel thither,
> And see the children sport upon the shore.
> And hear the mighty waters rolling evermore.

We do have that sense of infinity, we do hear the "mighty waters rolling evermore," we do long for the assurance of immortality, but the question is, How do we go about affirming that reality?

The messages of death answer by seducing us into false affirmations of that longing. They promise life, but give death. They guarantee freedom, but make us slaves. The messages of death urge us to fulfill infinite longings with finite things.

Do you have an infinite longing for security? Fulfill it, then, by making yourself as materially secure as possible, says the messenger of Death. Amass a fortune, gain the world, for that is the way to save your soul and make it impregnable. To be psychologically secure, never entrust yourself to anyone, take no risks, close yourself off, do not let yourself be vulnerable, cover your feelings, allow no one to get too close, not even your husband or wife. Mask your true emotions, show the world you are as psychologically secure as the Rock of Gibraltar. And then people wonder why their lives are burdensome and boring, and hard as stone. They build fortresses around themselves, dig wide, deep moats, and pull up the drawbridges of their souls.

But how different the gospel of life. Generating life and love within, it lowers the drawbridge and sends the self out to others. Upon hearing the royal herald announce the good news of God's eternal love, the self leaves its ego-throne of hubris or pride, and goes out to serve rather than to be served. Secure now in the knowledge of God's acceptance, the soul starts to tear down the fortress walls of fear and hostility to mingle freely and lovingly among the people.

By contrast the message of death draws the self in upon the self in a vain effort for self-induced immortality. The message of death passes out deceitful awards and titles to the self, reassuring the self it will be remembered forever in posterity, that the corporation or firm or college or church or family will stand forever as a tribute to the greatness of the self—myself.

But the gospel of life lures us away from that tawdry idolatry to the object of Michelangelo's art. The gospel inspires and ignites our imagination and infinite longings in Brahm's *German Requiem* or Mahler's Resurrection Symphony. The gospel of life causes us to break out into the exultant joy of Handel's *Messiah:*

THE MESSAGE OF DEATH VS. THE GOSPEL OF LIFE

"Hallelujah! Hallelujah! The Lord God Omnipotent Reigneth!" Your selfish self does not reign. My selfish self does not reign. Death does *not* sit upon the throne in all his deceptive, selfish glory. The Lord God, in all his humble, unselfish, majesterial love, reigns.

That is why the whole Western world has broken out in ecstatic music and poetry, literature and art. It is celebrating the gospel of life. It fills its libraries with books inspired by Jesus. Hospitals and orphanages, colleges and retirement homes, churches and service institutions by the thousands take their mighty impulse from his eternal heart of love and life.

But let Nietzsche's nihilism come to full flower, and you get a Hitler. Let Marx's materialism blossom, and you get a Stalin. Allow an unchecked scientism to bloom, and you get an American technocratic state where machines and computers are supreme, where efficiency and technique replace human freedom and feeling. Let Schopenhauer's despair run its graceless course, and you have a massive death wish, a tendency toward racial suicide.

But the gospel of life—how different! Rather than running from death, it looks it squarely in the face and says with preacher-poet John Donne:

> Death be not proud, though some have called thee
> Mighty and dreadful, for thou art not so,
> For those whom thou think'st thou dost overthrow,
> Die not, poor death, nor yet canst thou kill me.

PUTTING YOUR LIFE ON THE LINE

> One short sleep past, we wake eternally,
> And death shall be no more; death, thou shalt die.

Confident of God, the gospel of life finds it unnecessary to prop up the eternity of the soul with enticements of the material world. Assured of eternal value, the soul no longer is obsessed with producing eternal happiness out of the temporal. Paradoxically, the gospel of life liberates a man from slavery to the temporal, thus giving him freedom to enjoy it even more. It is the divine irony. When we lose our lives for the sake of the gospel, we find them. When we deny ourselves for Christ's sake, we sense the greatest fulfillment. When we seek first God's kingdom and his righteousness, the other things needful for a happy life are added to us.

We see a similar thing in the classroom. Many students go to college determined to impress the professors with their knowledge and intelligence. And paradoxically, the more the neophyte student asserts his knowledge and intelligence, the more he rests on his high school laurels, the less he is really able to enter into the fullest experience of the new truth college is wanting to give him. His intellectual growth is arrested, his spiritual development retarded, and his soul stunted. Consequently, in his defensive arrogance he tries to give eternal meaning to temporal knowledge. The conceit of his past closes him off to the limitless

THE MESSAGE OF DEATH VS. THE GOSPEL OF LIFE

potential of his future. His satisfaction with high school success sets him up for college failure.

The message of death always is seductive. It lures us toward self-satisfaction and self-righteousness, whereas the gospel of life keeps opening us up to the universe with all its newness and truth. Death's message leads to rigidity, inflexibility, atrophy, and despair. But God's gospel of resurrection brings us to exciting growth and development of our potential.

III

Third, the *gospel of life takes us beyond the temporary defeat of death to eternal victory.*

One test of whether we believe more in death than in life is the kind of hero we honor. Observe the statues we erect—mostly in honor of soldiers who gave their lives in death for great causes. We applaud the Sauls who have killed their thousands and Davids who have killed their tens of thousands. But what about missionaries who have given their entire lives to others, helping them out of ignorance, fear, and superstition, bringing them the gospel of life? What about hundreds of medical and technical and agricultural people who distribute medicine, food, and knowledge so that others might live more completely?

After forty years of service abroad, a retiring missionary was returning home on the same ship as an Army general. As the ship pulled into the dock, a huge crowd gathered and began cheering. Tears came to the missionary's eyes. In his long years in a remote part of the world, he often wondered if it really mattered, if anyone really cared. He had educated old and young, taught them how to read and write. When death had come, he stood by the families in long hours of grieving. When disease struck, or famine threatened, he often was an agent of mercy. Patiently he worked to release the people's minds from superstition. Child sacrifice ceased, cannibalism stopped, tribal warfare abated, and a life of wholesome cleanliness and joy often ensued.

Sometimes sick and lonely and frequently weary, the devoted missionary and his wife knew deep discouragement from time to time. There was great joy and satisfaction in their selfless work; nevertheless, they often wondered if it mattered to anyone else, if anyone remembered them and appreciated what they had done.

Therefore, when they came into the dock, their hearts filled with intense emotion and tears streamed down their wrinkled, kindly faces as they stood arm in arm, waving to the crowd. They were coming home. The people had remembered. They did care. Their selfless life of love and giving had been appreciated.

But as the gangplank was lowered, the battle-ribboned, many-medaled general was first off and a large cheer went up from the crowd as they carried him off on their shoulders. He had been grandly victorious in a battle which had involved some of the

THE MESSAGE OF DEATH VS. THE GOSPEL OF LIFE

missionary's own people—people he had loved and nurtured to wholesome life for forty years. And in one brief battle their lives were gone, snuffed out in senseless rage.

The missionary and his wife had tears of a different kind now as they made their silent, lonely way down the gangplank. And it was then he heard it, a voice which seemed to permeate the air, a gentle voice which said, "Don't despair, my friends, you're not home yet, you're not home yet."

So to all those devoting themselves to causes of justice and integrity in business and profession while the crooked and unjust seem to succeed with applause; to all those who are practicing charity, and thinking of others in a thousand ways big and little, while the greedy egoists gain the limelight; and to all those who are weary in well-doing, wondering about the rewards of the righteous life while the wicked prosper, the Lord of life says, "Don't despair my friends. You're not home yet."